AF796670

When a Storm Comes Up

By Allan Fowler

Consultants
Robert L. Hillerich, Professor Emeritus,
Bowling Green State University, Bowling Green, Ohio;
Consultant, Pinellas County Schools, Florida

Lynne Kepler, Educational Consultant

Fay Robinson, Child Development Specialist

Harcourt
SCHOOL PUBLISHERS

Visit The Learning Site!
www.harcourtschool.com

This edition is published by special arrangement with Children's Press, an imprint of Scholastic Library Publishing, Inc.

Grateful acknowledgment is made to Children's Press, an imprint of Scholastic Library Publishing, Inc., for permission to reprint *When a Storm Comes Up* by Allan Fowler. Text copyright 1995 by Childrens Press®, Inc.

Printed in China

ISBN 10 0-15-352482-0
ISBN 13 978-0-15-352482-0

7 8 9 10 0940 15 14 13 12 11 10 09

It feels good to be out in the sunshine on a warm day.

But the weather can't
be nice all the time.

In fact, you should be glad it sometimes rains.

Nothing could grow without rain — no fruits or vegetables, no trees or grass or flowers.

A light rain is called
a drizzle.

A little heavier rain is a shower.

And if it's really pouring?
That's a rainstorm.

When the sky becomes very dark, a thunderstorm could be on its way.

Even before the heavy rain reaches you, you might see flashes of lightning and hear deep, rolling thunder.

Lightning can be dangerous, so you'd better get indoors!

Does it snow a lot where you live? After a snowstorm, it's fun to go sledding . . .

or to build a snowman . . .
or to have a snowball fight.

But it's not fun for the people who must shovel paths in the snow so they can leave their houses . . .

or who must dig their cars out of the snow. A storm that brings this much snow is called a blizzard.

Some storms bring sleet,
a mixture of rain and snow.

You have to walk very
carefully, because sleet
can make the sidewalks
icy and slippery.

In a hailstorm, raindrops
freeze into ice before
they reach the ground.
Hail can be as big as this.

But don’t worry,
hailstones are almost
always much smaller.

Among the worst kinds of storms are hurricanes and tornados. A hurricane forms over the ocean.

When it reaches land, the winds may be so strong that they blow trees down . . .

the rains so heavy that
they cause floods . . .

the waves so high that
they wash houses and
sand beaches into the sea.

A tornado forms over land.
The winds whirl around in
a tall, funnel-shaped column.

Cars, roofs, even entire houses can be sucked up off the ground by a tornado.

The government has a weather service that works to learn when a hurricane or tornado is forming and which way it is going.

The weather service tries to warn the people who live along the storm's path in time for them to leave the area or take shelter.

In this way, many lives are saved. But nothing can stop a tornado or a hurricane from causing damage to property and to the land.

So next time it's raining a little too hard for you to go out and play . . .

be thankful that it's just
an ordinary storm.

Words You Know

thunderstorm

snowstorm

hurricane

tornado

lightning

drizzle

sleet

blizzard

hailstones

hail

Index

About the Author

Allan Fowler is a free-lance writer with a background in advertising. Born in New York, he lives in Chicago now and enjoys traveling.

Photo Credits

©Cameramann International, Ltd.–26

H. Armstrong Roberts–©J. Whitmer, 8, 22; ©V. Clevenger, 14; ©Camerique, 21

©Greg Stumpf–24, 30 (bottom right)

PhotoEdit–©Robert Brenner, 6; ©Richard Hutchings, 13; ©M. Richards, 23; ©Tony Freeman, 29

Root Resources–©Kathy Kohout, 18, 31 (bottom left)

Tom Stack & Associates–©J. Lotter, 4; ©Charlie Palek, 31 (center right)

SuperStock International, Inc.–©W. Gontscharoff, 3; ©Tom Rosenthal, 12; ©Frank Wood, 16, 31 (center left); ©Pedro Luis Raota, 28

Tony Stone Images–©Peter Pearson, 9; ©Barbara Filet, 31 (top left)

Unicorn Stock Photos–©James L. Fly, Cover; ©Sabrina Turner, 5; ©Tom McCarthy, 7, 31 (top right); ©Betts Anderson, 11, 30 (top left), 31 (bottom right); ©V.E. Horne, 15; ©Doris Brookes, 19; ©Terry Barner, 25; ©Karen Holsinger Mullen, 30 (top right)

Valan–©C. Malazrewicz, 20, 30 (bottom left)

COVER: Storm with lightning